500 EMERGING START UP IDEAS FOR NEW INDIA

DR DHEERAJ MEHROTRA

Contents

PREFACE

India is witnessing an entrepreneurial revolution, fueled by innovation, technology, and a growing ecosystem of young minds eager to disrupt traditional industries. As one of the world's fastest-growing economies, India provides immense opportunities for startups across various sectors, from artificial intelligence and green energy to education and healthcare.

The government's initiatives like Startup India, Digital India, and Atmanirbhar Bharat have further encouraged a culture of entrepreneurship, making it easier for aspiring founders to turn their dreams into reality. However, the biggest challenge for many is identifying the right business idea that is relevant, scalable, and sustainable in the long term. This book, **"500 Emerging Start-Up Ideas for New India,"** is a blueprint for aspiring entrepreneurs looking to start their journey. It provides innovative business ideas that align with India's evolving needs, leveraging technology, digital transformation, and market gaps. Whether you are a college graduate, working professional, investor, or an aspiring entrepreneur, this book will help spark inspiration and guide you towards a successful venture. The future of New India lies in entrepreneurship, and this book is a step towards building that future—one idea at a time.

Welcome to the start-up revolution!

www.authordheerajmehrotra.com

I

Start Up Ideas

India is a land of opportunities, with a rapidly growing economy, a young population, and increasing digital adoption. Here are innovative start-up ideas that cater to the needs and aspirations of New India:

1. **Drone Travel Photography Services:** *A service that provides travelers with professional drone photography and videography of their trips, capturing stunning aerial views. Offers unique and memorable travel keepsakes, Appeals to social media-savvy travelers.*

2. Online Coding Bootcamps: *Affordable coding courses for students and professionals.*

3. Vernacular E-Learning Platforms: *Education in regional languages.*

4. STEM Kits for Kids: *DIY science and engineering kits for children.*

5. Career Counseling Apps: *Personalized career guidance for students.*

6. Skill Development for Rural Youth: *Vocational training in farming, crafts, and trades.*

7. Gamified Learning Apps: *Interactive educational games for kids.*

8. AI-Powered Tutoring: *Personalized tutoring using artificial intelligence.*

9. Financial Literacy Programs: *Teach budgeting, investing, and saving to young adults.*

10. Online Exam Preparation Platforms: *Affordable test prep for competitive exams.*

11. Adult Education Platforms: *Lifelong learning for professionals.*

12. Health and Wellness

13. *Telemedicine for Rural Areas:* Affordable healthcare access via video consultations.

14. *Mental Health Apps:* Counseling and therapy for stress and anxiety.

15. *Ayurveda and Wellness Products:* Organic and traditional health products.

16. *Fitness Apps for Seniors:* Tailored exercise routines for the elderly.

17. *Meal Planning Services:* Customized diet plans for fitness enthusiasts.

18. *Health Monitoring Wearables:* Affordable devices for tracking vitals.

19. *Women's Health Platforms:* Focus on menstrual health, pregnancy, and postpartum care.

20. *Online Pharmacy Delivery:* Fast and reliable medicine delivery.

21. *Yoga and Meditation Apps:* Guided sessions for stress relief.

22. Health Insurance Comparison Platforms: Help users find the best insurance plans.

23. Carbon-Neutral Dining: It calculates each meal's carbon footprint and offsets it by investing in renewable energy projects.

24. Agri-Tech Marketplaces: Connect farmers with buyers directly.

25. Drone-Based Farming Solutions: Crop monitoring and spraying using drones.

26. Organic Farming Consultancy: Help farmers transition to organic practices.

27. Farm Equipment Rental Services: Affordable access to machinery.

28. Weather Forecasting Apps: Hyper-local weather updates for farmers.

29. Cold Storage Solutions: Reduce post-harvest losses for perishable goods.

30. Hydroponics and Vertical Farming: Urban farming solutions.

31. Livestock Management Apps: *Track and manage livestock health.*

32. Farm-to-Table Delivery Services: *Deliver fresh produce to urban consumers.*

33. Agricultural Waste Recycling: *Convert farm waste into valuable products.*

34. Sustainability and Green Tech

35. Solar Energy Solutions: *Affordable solar panels for homes and businesses.*

36. E-Waste Recycling: *Collect and recycle electronic waste.*

37. Eco-Friendly Packaging: *Sustainable packaging for businesses.*

38. Water Purification Systems: *Affordable solutions for rural areas.*

39. Electric Vehicle Charging Stations: *Build a network of EV charging points.*

40. Upcycled Fashion: *Create trendy clothing from recycled materials.*

41. Composting Services: Convert kitchen waste into compost.

42. Green Building Consultancy: Eco-friendly construction solutions.

53. Carbon Footprint Tracking Apps: Help individuals and businesses reduce emissions.

44. Bamboo-Based Products: Sustainable alternatives to plastic.

45. Fintech and Financial Inclusion

46. Micro-Lending Platforms: Small loans for entrepreneurs and farmers.

47. Digital Wallets for Rural India: Easy payment solutions for the unbanked.

48. Investment Apps for Beginners: Simplify stock market investing.

49. Insurance for Gig Workers: Affordable coverage for delivery and ride-sharing workers.

50. Financial Literacy Apps: Teach budgeting and saving to young adults.

51. Crowdfunding Platforms: Support social causes and start-ups.

52. Gold Investment Apps: Digitize gold savings and investments.

53. Peer-to-Peer Lending: Connect borrowers with individual lenders.

54. Expense Tracking Apps: Help users manage their finances.

55. Blockchain-Based Payment Solutions: Secure and transparent transactions.

56. Technology and Innovation

57. AI-Powered Chatbots: Customer service solutions for businesses.

58. Cybersecurity Solutions: Protect SMEs from cyber threats.

59. AR/VR Training Platforms: Immersive learning for industries.

60. IoT-Based Home Automation: Smart home devices for Indian households.

61. Robotics for Manufacturing: Affordable automation solutions for SMEs.

62. Cloud-Based ERP Systems: Streamline business operations.

63. Voice Search Optimization: Help businesses adapt to voice search trends.

64. AI-Driven Recruitment Platforms: Simplify hiring for companies.

65. Data Analytics for SMEs: Help small businesses make data-driven decisions.

66. 5G-Based Solutions: Develop apps and services for 5G networks.

67. E-Commerce and Retail

68. Hyperlocal Delivery Services: Fast delivery of groceries and essentials.

69. Handmade Product Marketplaces: Support local artisans and craftsmen.

70. Subscription Box Services: Curated boxes for beauty, snacks, or books.

71. Resale Platforms for Fashion: Second-hand clothing and accessories.

72. Customized Gift Services: Personalized gifts for special occasions.

73. Rental Platforms for Electronics: Rent laptops, cameras, and gadgets.

74. Online Thrift Stores: Affordable pre-owned items.

75. D2C (Direct-to-Consumer) Brands: Build brands that sell directly to customers.

76. Virtual Try-On Apps: Augmented reality for fashion and accessories.

77. E-Commerce for Rural Artisans: Help rural artisans reach global markets.

78. Travel and Tourism

79. Eco-Tourism Platforms: Promote sustainable travel experiences.

80. Adventure Travel Packages: *Curated trips for thrill-seekers.*

81. Heritage Tourism: *Showcase India's cultural and historical sites.*

82. Homestay Aggregators: *Connect travelers with local hosts.*

83. Travel Planning Apps: *Personalized itineraries for tourists.*

84. Local Experience Platforms: *Unique experiences like cooking classes or village tours.*

85. Luggage Storage Solutions: *Safe storage for travelers in cities.*

86. Road Trip Planning Apps: *Help users plan road trips across India.*

87. Sustainable Travel Gear: *Eco-friendly luggage and accessories.*

88. Virtual Travel Experiences: *Explore destinations through VR.*

89. Social Impact and Community Development

90. Crowdsourced Disaster Relief: Coordinate aid during natural disasters.

91. Women's Safety Apps: Emergency alerts and safety features.

92. Community Waste Management: Organize waste collection and recycling.

93. Rural Healthcare Camps: Mobile clinics for underserved areas.

94. Digital Literacy Programs: Teach digital skills to rural communities.

95. Crowdfunding for Social Causes: Support education, healthcare, and more.

96. Volunteer Matching Platforms: Connect volunteers with NGOs.

97. Clean Water Initiatives: Provide affordable water purification solutions.

98. Affordable Housing Solutions: Low-cost housing for urban poor.

99. Animal Welfare Platforms: Support for stray animals and pets.

100. Emergency Assistance App : An app that provides 24/ 7 emergency assistance, including medical help, legal support, and evacuation services, for travelers worldwide. Why It's Great: Enhances traveler safety and peace of mind. Fills a critical gap in the travel industry.

101. Develop a platform that connects patients with healthcare professionals for remote consultations, making healthcare more accessible.

102. Create an online learning platform that offers courses in various subjects, catering to students of all ages.

103. Sustainable Packaging: Start a business that produces biodegradable and eco-friendly packaging solutions for e-commerce and retail.

104. Smart Home Automation: Design and install smart home systems that enhance security, energy efficiency, and convenience for homeowners.

105. Organic Farming: Launch an organic farm that supplies fresh produce to local markets and restaurants, promoting healthy eating.

106. Virtual Reality Experiences: Develop VR experiences for education, training, or entertainment, providing

immersive learning and engagement.

107. Mobile Payment Solutions: Create a mobile payment app that simplifies transactions for consumers and small businesses.

108. Fitness Tech: Design wearable fitness devices that track health metrics and provide personalized workout plans.

109. Mental Health Apps: Develop an app that offers mental health resources, including therapy sessions, meditation guides, and support communities.

110. Renewable Energy Solutions: Start a company that provides solar panel installations and energy-efficient solutions for homes and businesses.

111. Food Waste Management: Create a service that collects food waste from restaurants and households for composting or recycling.

112. Personalized Nutrition: Launch a platform that offers personalized meal plans and nutrition advice based on individual health data.

113. E-Commerce for Local Artisans: Build an online marketplace that connects local artisans with consumers, promoting handmade and unique products.

114. Subscription Box Services: Start a subscription box service that curates products based on specific interests, such as beauty, fitness, or books.

115. Digital Marketing Agency: Offer digital marketing services to small businesses, helping them establish an online presence and reach their target audience.

116. Home Cleaning Services: Create a reliable home cleaning service that uses eco-friendly products and offers flexible scheduling.

117. Pet Care Services: Launch a pet care business that provides pet owners grooming, walking, and boarding services.

118. Language Learning Apps: Develop an app that helps users learn new languages through interactive lessons and real-life practice.

119. Online Grocery Delivery: Start an online grocery delivery service focusing on fresh produce and local products.

120. Remote Work Solutions: Create tools and platforms that enhance productivity and collaboration for remote teams.

121. Elderly Care Services: Establish a service that provides in-home care and companionship for the elderly.

122. Blockchain Solutions: Develop blockchain-based applications for secure transactions and data management across various industries.

123. Influencer Marketing Platform: Create a platform that connects brands with influencers for effective marketing campaigns.

124. Travel Planning Services: Launch a travel planning service that offers personalized itineraries and experiences for travelers.

125. Smart Agriculture: Develop technology solutions that optimize farming practices through data analytics and IoT.

126. Custom Apparel: Start a business that offers custom-designed clothing and accessories for individuals and companies.

127. Mobile Car Wash: Create a mobile car wash service that provides convenient cleaning solutions at customers' locations.

128. Digital Health Records: Develop a platform that securely allows patients to manage and share their health records.

129. Online Therapy: Launch an online therapy platform that connects users with licensed therapists for virtual sessions.

130. Event Planning Services: Start an event planning business specialising in corporate events, weddings, and private parties.

131. Eco-Friendly Cleaning Products: Create eco-friendly cleaning products that are safe for homes and the environment.

132. Crowdfunding Platform: Develop a crowdfunding platform that supports startups and social causes.

133. Home Renovation Services: Launch a home renovation business that offers design and construction services.

134. Digital Art Marketplace: Create an online marketplace for digital artists to sell their work and connect with buyers.

135. Personal Finance Apps: Develop an app that helps users manage their finances, track expenses, and save money.

136. Smart Wearables for Kids: Design wearable devices for children that promote safety and health monitoring.

137. Urban Farming Solutions: Start a business that provides solutions for urban farming, such as vertical gardens and hydroponics.

138. Online Tutoring: Create a platform that connects students with tutors for personalized learning experiences.

139. Mobile Health Clinics: Launch a mobile health clinic that provides medical services to underserved communities.

140. Digital Content Creation: Start a content creation agency that produces videos, blogs, and social media content for brands.

141. AI-Powered Customer Support: Develop an AI-driven customer support platform that enhances user experience and satisfaction.

142. Virtual Fitness Classes: Create a platform that offers live and on-demand fitness classes for users to join from home.

143. Home Gardening Kits: Launch a business that sells home gardening kits with everything needed to grow plants indoors or outdoors.

144. Online Marketplace for Second-Hand Goods: Develop a platform for buying and selling second-hand items, promoting sustainability and reducing waste.

145. Digital Identity Verification: Create a service that offers secure digital identity verification for businesses and *individuals.*

146. Personalized Gift Services: *Start a business that curates and delivers personalized gifts for special occasions.*

147. Smart Waste Management: *Develop an intelligent waste management system that optimizes collection routes and recycling processes.*

148. Online Cooking Classes: *Launch a platform that offers cooking classes with professional chefs for home cooks.*

149. Home Office Solutions: *Create a business that provides ergonomic furniture and accessories for home office setups.*

150. Community-Based Tourism: *Start a tourism business that focuses on community engagement and cultural experiences.*

151. Digital Nomad Services: *Develop services that cater to digital nomads, such as co-working spaces and travel planning.*

152. Subscription-Based Fitness Programs: *Launch a subscription service that offers access to various fitness programs and resources.*

153. Smart Water Management: *Create technology solutions that optimize water usage and conservation for* *households and businesses.*

154. Online Mental Health Support Groups: *Develop a platform that connects individuals with mental health support groups and resources.*

155. Personalized Skincare: *Start a skincare brand offering personalized products based on skin types and concerns.*

156. Remote Learning Tools for Schools: *Create tools that enhance remote learning experiences for educators and students.*

157. Digital Marketing for Nonprofits: *Offer digital marketing services specifically tailored for nonprofit organizations.*

158. Home-Based Food Businesses: *Launch a platform that supports home-based food entrepreneurs in selling their products.*

159. Virtual Reality Therapy: *Develop VR therapy solutions for mental health treatment and rehabilitation.*

160. Online Fitness Challenges: *Create a platform that hosts fitness challenges and competitions for users to participate in.*

161. Smart Fitness Equipment: *Design fitness equipment that integrates technology for tracking workouts and* progress.

162. AI-Powered Recruitment: Develop an AI-driven recruitment platform that streamlines companies' hiring process.

163. Online Art Classes: Launch a platform that offers art classes for all skill levels, taught by professional artists.

164. Mobile App Development: Start a mobile app development agency that creates custom apps for businesses.

165. Eco-Friendly Fashion: Create a fashion brand that focuses on sustainable materials and ethical production practices.

166. Online Language Exchange: Develop a platform that connects language learners for practice and cultural exchange.

167. Smart Fitness Studios: Launch a fitness studio that incorporates technology for personalized training experiences.

168. Digital Asset Management: Create a platform for businesses to manage and organize their digital assets efficiently.

169. Online Marketplace for Local Food: Start a marketplace that connects consumers with local farmers and food producers.

170. Virtual Reality Travel Experiences: Develop VR travel experiences that allow users to explore destinations from home.

171. Home Security Solutions: Create a business that offers smart home security systems for residential properties.

172. Online Parenting Resources: Launch a platform that provides resources and support for parents, including articles and forums.

173. Digital Wellness Programs: Develop wellness programs that promote mental and physical health in the workplace.

174. Customizable Home Decor: Start a business that offers customizable home decor products for consumers.

175. Online Fitness Coaching: Create a platform that connects users with certified fitness coaches for personalized training.

176. Smart Kitchen Appliances: Design kitchen appliances that integrate technology for convenience and efficiency.

177. Online Community for Entrepreneurs: Launch a platform that connects entrepreneurs for networking, *support, and collaboration.*

178. Personalized Travel Planning: Develop a travel planning service that creates customized itineraries based on user preferences.

179. Digital Learning Resources for Teachers: Create a platform that offers teaching resources and tools for educators.

180. Smart Health Monitoring Devices: Design health monitoring devices that track vital signs and provide real-time feedback.

181. Online Marketplace for Handmade Goods: Start a marketplace that connects artisans with consumers looking for unique handmade products.

182. Virtual Reality Training for Professionals: Develop VR training programs for professionals in various industries.

183. Home Renovation Consulting: Launch a consulting service that helps homeowners plan and execute renovation projects.

184. Digital Marketing Analytics: Create a platform that provides analytics and insights for digital marketing campaigns.

185. Online Fitness Communities: Develop a platform that connects fitness enthusiasts for support and motivation.

186. Smart City Solutions: Start a business that provides technology solutions for urban planning and development.

187. Online Marketplace for Vintage Goods: Create a platform for buying and selling vintage and antique items.

188. Personalized Learning Platforms: Develop a learning platform that adapts to individual learning styles and paces.

189. Mobile App for Local Services: Launch an app that connects users with local service providers, such as plumbers and electricians.

190. Digital Art Therapy: Create a platform that offers digital art therapy sessions for mental health support.

191. Online Marketplace for Eco-Friendly Products: Start a marketplace that focuses on sustainable and eco-friendly products.

192. Smart Fitness Challenges: Develop a platform that hosts fitness challenges with gamification elements.

193. Online Career Coaching: Launch a career coaching service that helps individuals navigate their professional paths.

194. Digital Tools for Remote Collaboration: Create tools that enhance collaboration and communication for remote teams.

195. Personalized Home Cleaning Services: Start a cleaning service that tailors its offerings to individual client needs.

196. Online Marketplace for Local Crafts: Develop a platform that connects consumers with local craftsmen and artisans.

197. Smart Energy Solutions: Create technology solutions that optimize energy consumption for households and businesses.

198. Virtual Reality Fitness Programs: Launch fitness programs that utilize virtual reality for immersive workouts.

199. Online Platform for Skill Sharing: Develop a platform that connects individuals for skill-sharing and learning opportunities.

200. Smart Pet Products: Create innovative products for pets that enhance their health and well-being.

201. AI-Powered Career Matching: Match students with careers based on skills and interests.

202. Virtual Reality Classrooms: Immersive learning experiences for schools.

203. Parenting Workshops: Teach modern parenting techniques.

204. Language Learning Apps for Kids: Fun and interactive ways to learn new languages.

205. Online Internship Platforms: Connect students with companies for virtual internships.

206. Special Education Tools: Apps and tools for children with learning disabilities.

207. Teacher Training Platforms: Upskill teachers with modern teaching methods.

208. Student Loan Counseling: Help students navigate education loans.

209. Peer Tutoring Platforms: Connect students for peer-to-peer learning.

210. Digital Libraries: *Affordable access to e-books and academic resources.*

211. Health and Wellness- Personalized Nutrition Plans: *Tailored diets based on DNA or health data.*

212. Mental Health Chatbots: *AI-driven support for stress and anxiety.*

213. Fitness Challenges Apps: *Gamify fitness with challenges and rewards.*

214. Health Wearables for Kids: *Track children's health and activity levels.*

215. Online Therapy for Couples: *Counseling for relationship issues.*

216. Holistic Wellness Centers: *Combine yoga, meditation, and nutrition.*

217. Health Data Analytics: *Help individuals analyze their health trends.*

218. Sleep Improvement Apps: *Tools to track and improve sleep quality.*

219. Virtual Fitness Classes: Live or on-demand workouts for all levels.

220. Health Tourism Platforms: Curated wellness retreats in India.

221. Agriculture and Rural Development

222. Farm-to-Consumer Apps: Directly connect farmers with consumers.

223. Soil Testing Kits: Affordable kits to analyze soil health.

224. Agri-Tourism Platforms: Promote farm stays and rural experiences.

225. Livestock Health Monitoring: Wearables for animal health tracking.

226. Crop Insurance Platforms: Simplify insurance for farmers.

227. Agricultural Drones for Small Farms: Affordable drone solutions.

228. Farm Labor Marketplaces: Connect farmers with laborers.

229. Organic Certification Services: Help farmers get certified.

230. Water Management Solutions: Smart irrigation systems.

231. Rural E-Commerce Hubs: Enable rural artisans to sell online.

232. Sustainability and Green Tech

233. Solar-Powered Appliances: Affordable solar gadgets for homes.

234. Plastic Alternatives: Develop biodegradable packaging.

235. Green Energy Consulting: Help businesses adopt renewable energy.

236. Urban Gardening Kits: Promote gardening in small spaces.

237. Waste-to-Energy Solutions: Convert waste into usable energy.

238. Eco-Friendly Cleaning Products: Non-toxic and sustainable cleaners.

239. Carbon Credit Marketplaces: Help businesses trade carbon credits.

240. Sustainable Fashion Rental: Rent high-end sustainable clothing.

241. Green Transportation Apps: Promote carpooling and cycling.

242. Reusable Packaging Solutions: For e-commerce and food delivery.

243. Fintech and Financial Inclusion: Digital Banking for Rural India: Mobile-first banking solutions.

244. Micro-Insurance Platforms: Affordable insurance for low-income groups.

245. Expense Splitting Apps: Simplify group payments and bill splitting.

246. Financial Planning for Women: Tailored advice for women's financial goals.

247. Blockchain-Based Land Records: Secure and transparent property records.

248. *Crowdfunding for Start-Ups:* Help early-stage businesses raise funds.

249. *Digital Gold Savings Apps:* Encourage gold savings among millennials.

250. *AI-Driven Credit Scoring:* Assess creditworthiness using alternative data.

251. *Financial Literacy for Kids:* Teach children about money management.

252. *Peer-to-Peer Insurance:* Community-based insurance models.

253. *Technology and Innovation- AI-Powered Legal Assistants:* Simplify legal research and documentation.

254. *Smart Home Security Systems:* Affordable and easy-to-install solutions.

255. *AR/VR for Real Estate:* Virtual property tours for buyers.

256. *IoT-Based Health Devices:* Remote monitoring for patients.

257. *AI-Driven Content Creation: Tools for writers, designers, and marketers.*

258. *Cybersecurity for SMEs: Protect small businesses from cyber threats.*

259. *Voice-Activated Assistants: Customized for Indian languages.*

260. *Robotics for Elderly Care: Assistive robots for seniors.*

261. *Data Privacy Solutions: Help businesses comply with data laws.*

262. *AI-Powered Market Research: Analyze consumer trends and behavior.*

263. *Gamification: Reward customers with points for sustainable actions, like bringing their containers or choosing plant-based meals.*

264. *Hyperlocal Artisan Marketplaces: Promote local crafts and products.*

265. *Subscription-Based Grocery Delivery: Weekly essentials delivered to your door.*

266. Customized Apparel Brands: *Personalized clothing and accessories.*

267. Online Thrift Stores for Kids: *Affordable second-hand children's items.*

268. E-Commerce for Handicrafts: *Connect artisans with global buyers.*

269. Virtual Pop-Up Stores: *Temporary online stores for brands.*

270. Eco-Friendly Fashion Brands: *Sustainable and ethical clothing.*

271. Rental Platforms for Luxury Items: *Rent designer clothes, bags, and jewelry.*

272. AI-Powered Shopping Assistants: *Personalized product recommendations.*

273. Direct-to-Consumer Beauty Brands: *Affordable and high-quality cosmetics.*

274. Travel and Tourism- Cultural Immersion Tours: *Deep dive into local traditions and customs.*

275. Sustainable Travel Agencies: Eco-friendly travel packages.

276. Adventure Travel Gear Rentals: Affordable gear for outdoor enthusiasts.

277. Virtual Travel Guides: AI-powered guides for tourists.

278. Luxury Camping Experiences: Glamping in scenic locations.

279. Pilgrimage Tourism Platforms: Curated trips for spiritual journeys.

280. Local Food Tours: Explore regional cuisines with locals.

281. Travel Insurance Comparison: Find the best travel insurance plans.

282. Pet-Friendly Travel Services: Accommodations and tours for pet owners.

283. Digital Nomad Hubs: Co-living spaces for remote workers.

284. Addresses Global Challenges: *Tackles food waste, climate change, and the demand for transparency in the food industry.*

285. Crowdsourced Fundraising for Education: *Support underprivileged students.*

286. Women's Entrepreneurship Platforms: *Training and funding for women.*

287. Community Solar Projects: *Shared solar energy for villages.*

288. Digital Literacy for Seniors: *Teach elderly citizens to use smartphones.*

289. Rural Healthcare Delivery Drones: *Deliver medicines to remote areas.*

290. Crowdfunding for Farmers: *Support farmers during crises.*

291. Volunteer Tourism Platforms: *Combine travel with social impact.*

292. Clean Energy for Schools: *Solar-powered schools in rural areas.*

293. Affordable Sanitation Solutions: Low-cost toilets for rural households.

294. Animal Adoption Platforms: Connect shelters with potential adopters.

295. Entertainment and Media- Regional Language Podcasts: Podcasts in Indian languages.

296. Interactive Storytelling Apps: Choose-your-own-adventure stories.

297. Virtual Reality Concerts: Immersive music experiences.

298. Niche Streaming Services: Focus on genres like indie films or stand-up comedy.

299. Content Creation Tools for Influencers: Apps for editing and monetizing content.

300. Gaming Apps with Social Impact: Games that raise awareness about social issues.

301. Digital Art Galleries: Showcase and sell digital artwork.

302. Local News Aggregators: Hyperlocal news for communities.

303. AI-Powered Music Composition: Tools for creating original music.

304. Virtual Reality Fitness Games: Combine gaming with exercise.

305. AI-Powered Career Counseling: Personalized career guidance using AI.

306. Virtual Internship Platforms: Connect students with global companies.

307. Gamified Learning for Adults: Make upskilling fun and engaging.

308. Online Coding Competitions: Host coding challenges for students.

309. Language Learning for Professionals: Focus on business communication.

310. Virtual Science Fairs: Showcase student projects online.

311. Teacher Resource Marketplaces: Share lesson plans and teaching tools.

312. Student Mental Health Apps: Provide counseling and stress management.

313. Virtual Study Groups: Facilitate collaborative learning online.

314. AI-Powered Exam Prep: Personalized study plans for competitive exams.

315. Health and Wellness- Personalized Wellness Plans: Tailored health plans based on DNA.

316. Mental Health Retreats: Weekend getaways for stress relief.

317. Health Tracking for Seniors: Wearables to monitor elderly health.

318. Online Fitness Challenges: Community-driven fitness goals.

319. Holistic Health Subscriptions: Monthly boxes with wellness products.

320. AI-Powered Diet Plans: Customized nutrition based on health data.

321. Sleep Improvement Devices: Gadgets to enhance sleep quality.

322. Virtual Yoga Classes: Live or on-demand sessions for all levels.

323. Health Gamification Apps: Turn fitness into a game.

324. Telemedicine for Mental Health: Online therapy and counseling.

325. Agriculture and Rural Development- Farm-to-School Programs: Deliver fresh produce to schools.

326. Agri-Tech Weather Apps: Hyper-local weather forecasts for farmers.

327. Crop Insurance Platforms: Simplify insurance claims for farmers.

328. Farm Equipment Rental Apps: Affordable access to machinery.

329. Agricultural Drone Services: Crop monitoring and spraying.

330. Rural E-Commerce Platforms: Help artisans sell products online.

331. Organic Farming Consultancy: Guide farmers in transitioning to organic methods.

332. Farm Waste Management: Convert waste into biogas or compost.

333. Livestock Health Apps: Track and manage animal health.

334. Agri-Tourism Experiences: Farm stays and rural adventures.

335. Sustainability and Green Tech- Solar-Powered Gadgets: Affordable solar devices for homes.

336. Eco-Friendly Packaging: Sustainable alternatives to plastic.

337. Green Energy Crowdfunding: Fund renewable energy projects.

338. Urban Vertical Gardens: Grow food in small urban spaces.

339. Waste Collection Apps: Schedule pickups for recyclable waste.

340. Biodegradable Products: Eco-friendly alternatives to single-use items.

341. Carbon Offset Platforms: Help individuals offset their carbon footprint.

342. Sustainable Home Products: Eco-friendly furniture and decor.

343. Green Transportation Solutions: Promote electric bikes and scooters.

344. Water-Saving Devices: Smart gadgets to reduce water usage.

345. Fintech and Financial Inclusion- Digital Savings Groups: Community-based savings platforms.

346. Micro-Investment Apps: Allow small investments in stocks or mutual funds.

347. Financial Literacy for Teens: Teach money management to teenagers.

348. **Blockchain-Based Voting Systems:** Secure and transparent voting solutions.

349. AI-Powered Budgeting Tools: Help users manage their finances.

350. Crowdfunding for Medical Expenses: Support for healthcare costs.

351. Digital Gold Gifting: Send gold as gifts through apps.

352. Peer-to-Peer Lending for Education: Fund students' education.

353. Insurance for Freelancers: Tailored plans for gig workers.

354. Financial Planning for Seniors: Help retirees manage their savings.

355. Technology and Innovation - AI-Powered Resume Builders: Create professional resumes instantly.

356. Smart Home Energy Management: Optimize energy usage in homes.

357. AR/VR for Education: Immersive learning experiences.

358. IoT-Based Smart Farming: *Monitor crops and livestock remotely.*

359. AI-Driven Customer Support: *Chatbots for businesses.*

360. Cybersecurity for Individuals: *Protect personal data online.*

361. Voice-Activated Home Assistants: *Customized for Indian households.*

362. Robotics for Household Chores: *Affordable home robots.*

363. Data Analytics for Farmers: *Help farmers make data-driven decisions.*

364. AI-Powered Content Moderation: *Monitor and filter online content.*

365. E-Commerce and Retail- Customized Jewelry Brands: *Personalized designs for customers.*

366. Subscription-Based Pet Supplies: *Monthly deliveries for pet owners.*

367. E-Commerce for Handicrafts: *Promote traditional Indian crafts.*

368. *Virtual Try-On for Eyewear: AR-based glasses fitting.*

369. *Online Thrift Stores for Teens: Affordable second-hand fashion.*

370. *Eco-Friendly Baby Products: Sustainable diapers, toys, and clothing.*

371. *Rental Platforms for Party Supplies: Rent decorations and equipment.*

372. *AI-Powered Fashion Stylists: Personalized outfit recommendations.*

373. *Direct-to-Consumer Snack Brands: Healthy and affordable snacks.*

374. *Virtual Pop-Up Stores: Temporary online stores for brands.*

375. *Travel and Tourism- Cultural Exchange Platforms: Connect travelers with locals.*

376. *Sustainable Travel Gear: Eco-friendly luggage and accessories.*

377. Adventure Travel Insurance: Tailored plans for thrill-seekers.

378. Virtual Travel Guides: AI-powered guides for tourists.

379. Luxury Train Travel: Curated experiences on Indian railways.

380. Pilgrimage Tourism Apps: Plan spiritual journeys with ease.

381. Local Food Delivery for Tourists: Authentic meals delivered to hotels.

382. Travel Insurance Comparison: Find the best plans for your trip.

383. Pet-Friendly Travel Services: Accommodations and tours for pet owners.

384. Digital Nomad Hubs: Co-living spaces for remote workers.

385. Social Impact and Community Development-Crowdsourced Fundraising for Education: Support underprivileged students.

386. **Women's Entrepreneurship Platforms:** *Training and funding for women.*

387. **Community Solar Projects:** *Shared solar energy for villages.*

388. **Digital Literacy for Seniors:** *Teach elderly citizens to use smartphones.*

389. **Rural Healthcare Delivery Drones:** *Deliver medicines to remote areas.*

390. **Crowdfunding for Farmers:** *Support farmers during crises.*

391. **Volunteer Tourism Platforms:** *Combine travel with social impact.*

392. **Clean Energy for Schools:** *Solar-powered schools in rural areas.*

393. **Affordable Sanitation Solutions:** *Low-cost toilets for rural households.*

394. **Animal Adoption Platforms:** *Connect shelters with potential adopters.*

395. Entertainment and Media- Regional Language Podcasts: Podcasts in Indian languages.

396. Interactive Storytelling Apps: Choose-your-own-adventure stories.

397. Virtual Reality Concerts: Immersive music experiences.

398. Niche Streaming Services: Focus on genres like indie films or stand-up comedy.

399. Content Creation Tools for Influencers: Apps for editing and monetizing content.

400. Gaming Apps with Social Impact: Games that raise awareness about social issues.

401. Digital Art Galleries: Showcase and sell digital artwork.

402. Local News Aggregators: Hyperlocal news for communities.

403. AI-Powered Music Composition: Tools for creating original music.

404. Virtual Reality Fitness Games: Combine gaming with exercise.

405. Share behind-the-scenes videos of zero-waste kitchens and urban farms.

406. Collaborate with eco-conscious influencers and chefs.

407. Host events like "Zero-Waste Cooking Challenges" and "Farm-to-Table Dinners."

408. Reward customers with points for sustainable actions, like bringing their containers or choosing plant-based meals.

409. GreenPack – Reusable Packaging Network: A subscription-based service that provides reusable packaging for e-commerce and food delivery. Customers return the packaging after use, and it's cleaned and reused. Why It's Great: Reduces single-use plastic waste. Appeals to eco-conscious consumers and businesses.

410. SolarCharge – Portable Solar Chargers for Urban Dwellers: Compact, foldable solar chargers for smartphones and laptops, designed for urban commuters and travelers. Why It's Great: Promotes renewable energy use. Targets the growing demand for portable charging solutions.

411. EcoThreads – Sustainable Fashion Rental: A platform that rents high-quality, sustainable fashion items for special occasions or everyday wear. Why It's Great: Reduces textile waste and promotes circular fashion. Appeals to budget-conscious and eco-friendly consumers.

412. AquaHarvest – Rainwater Harvesting Kits for Homes: *Affordable, easy-to-install rainwater harvesting systems for urban and rural households. Why It's Great: Addresses water scarcity issues. Encourages sustainable water management.*

413. BioBricks – Building Materials from Agricultural Waste: *Eco-friendly bricks made from agricultural waste like rice husks and straw, used for construction. Why It's Great: Reduces agricultural waste and deforestation. Provides affordable, sustainable building materials.*

414. EcoRide – Electric Bike Sharing in Cities: *A network of electric bikes for short-distance commuting in urban areas, with solar-powered charging stations. Why It's Great: Reduces carbon emissions and traffic congestion. Promotes healthy and sustainable transportation.*

415. GreenGrocer – Zero-Waste Grocery Delivery: *An online grocery store that delivers reusable or compostable packaging products, focusing on local and organic produce. Why It's Great: Eliminates plastic waste and supports local farmers. Appeals to eco-conscious consumers.*

416. EcoCraft – Upcycled Home Decor: *A brand that creates stylish home decor items from upcycled materials like wood, glass, and fabric. Why It's Great: Reduces waste and promotes creativity. Targets the growing market for sustainable home products.*

417. CleanWave – Ocean Plastic Recycling: *A start-up that collects ocean plastic and transforms it into high-quality* *products like sunglasses, bags, and furniture. Why It's Great: Tackles ocean pollution and promotes recycling. Creates a positive environmental impact.*

418. EcoEats – Plant-Based Meal Kits: *Subscription-based meal kits featuring plant-based recipes and locally sourced, organic ingredients. Why It's Great: Promotes sustainable eating habits. Appeals to health-conscious and eco-friendly consumers.*

419. EcoClean – Non-Toxic Cleaning Products: *Develop and sell eco-friendly cleaning solutions made from natural ingredients.*

420. GreenGadgets – Repair and Refurbish Electronics: *Offer repair services and sell refurbished electronics to reduce e-waste.*

421. SolarSolutions – Solar-Powered Appliances: *Create affordable solar-powered gadgets like fans, lights, and chargers.*

422. EcoTravel – Sustainable Tourism Platform: *Curate eco-friendly travel experiences, including stays, tours, and activities.*

423. BioPack – Edible Packaging: *Develop edible packaging for snacks and beverages to eliminate plastic waste.*

424. EcoStay – Sustainable Accommodation Platform: *A booking platform that features eco-friendly hotels,* homestays, and resorts with verified sustainability certifications. Why It's Great: Appeals to eco-conscious travelers. Promotes responsible tourism.

425. LocalEats – Culinary Tourism App: An app that connects travelers with local food experiences, such as cooking classes, food tours, and home-cooked meals with locals. Why It's Great: Offers authentic cultural experiences. Supports local communities.

426. TravelMate – AI-Powered Travel Planner: An AI-driven platform that creates personalized travel itineraries based on user preferences, budget, and interests. Why It's Great: Saves time and enhances travel planning. Provides tailored recommendations.

427. AdventureHub – Curated Adventure Travel Packages: A platform offering curated adventure travel packages, including trekking, scuba diving, and wildlife safaris. Why It's Great: Targets thrill-seekers and adventure enthusiasts. Creates unforgettable experiences.

428. CultureConnect – Immersive Cultural Experiences: A service that connects travelers with local hosts for immersive cultural experiences, such as traditional dance lessons, craft workshops, and storytelling sessions. Why It's Great: Promotes cultural exchange and understanding. Supports local artisans and communities.

429. GreenTransit – Eco-Friendly Transportation Network: A platform that offers eco-friendly transportation options, such as electric bikes, solar-powered shuttles, and carpooling services. Why It's Great: Reduces carbon

emissions. Appeals to environmentally conscious travelers.

430. VirtualVoyage – VR Travel Experiences: *A virtual reality platform that allows users to explore destinations and attractions from the comfort of their homes. Why It's Great: Ideal for people who cannot travel physically. Offers a unique way to discover new places.*

431. TravelGuard – On-Demand Travel Insurance: *An app that offers flexible, on-demand travel insurance for specific activities, days, or trips. Why It's Great: Provides affordable and customizable insurance options. Appeals to budget-conscious travelers.*

432. PetFriendly – Travel Services for Pet Owners: *A platform that curates pet-friendly accommodations, activities, and transportation options for travelers with pets. Why It's Great: Addresses the growing demand for pet-friendly travel. Creates a niche market.*

433. SoloTraveler – Community for Solo Travelers: *A platform that connects solo travelers with like-minded individuals for group trips, meetups, and safety tips. Why It's Great: Builds a supportive community for solo travelers. Enhances safety and social experiences.*

434. HeritageTrails – Guided Historical Tours: *Offer guided tours of historical sites with expert storytellers.*

435. WellnessRetreats – Curated Wellness Getaways: Organize wellness retreats focused on yoga, meditation, and spa treatments.

436. TravelSwap – Home Exchange Platform: Allow travelers to swap homes with others for a unique and cost-effective stay.

437. LuggageFree – Door-to-Door Luggage Delivery: Provide hassle-free luggage delivery services for travelers.

438. LocalGuides – Hyperlocal Travel Guides: Create hyperlocal travel guides with insider tips and hidden gems.

439. After-School Activity Hub – Sports, music, dance, and arts coaching.

440. Student Counseling & Career Guidance – AI-based career guidance for students.

441. Internship & Job Placement Portal – Connecting students with internships.

442. Educational Travel Agency – Organizing educational tours and industrial visits.

443. College Admission Consulting – Helping students apply to top colleges abroad.

444. Scholarship & Grant Assistance Platform – Helping students find scholarships.

445. School Supplies E-commerce Store – Online marketplace for uniforms, books, and stationery.

446. Student Housing & PG Finder – Platform to find verified student accommodations.

447. Mental Health & Well-being App – Meditation, therapy, and student wellness programs.

448. University Merchandise & Apparel Store – Selling customized school/college merchandise.

449. Online Teacher Training Academy – Upskilling teachers with digital tools.

450. Freelance Teacher Marketplace – Connecting expert educators with schools.

451. AI-Powered Lesson Planning Tool – Automated lesson plan creation for teachers.

452. Teacher Community & Networking Platform – Professional networking for educators.

453. Classroom Resource Hub – Digital teaching materials, PPTs, lesson plans.

454. Teacher Coaching & Personality Development – Helping teachers enhance soft skills.

455. Eco-Friendly School Supplies – Sustainable stationery, uniforms, and books.

456. Smart Uniforms with GPS – Wearable tech for student safety.

457. School Cafeteria Automation – Pre-paid meal plans and digital ordering.

458. Waste Management Solutions for Schools – Recycling and eco-friendly waste disposal.

459. Solar Energy Solutions for Schools – Helping schools transition to green energy.

460. Affordable Digital Whiteboard Solutions – Low-cost smart classroom tech.

461. University Alumni Networking Platform – Connecting alumni and students.

462. College Event Ticketing Platform – Online ticketing for fests, workshops, and events.

463. AI-Powered Research Assistant – Helping students with thesis and projects.

464. Freelance Marketplace for Students – Connecting students with freelance gigs.

465. AI-Based Resume Builder for Students – Personalized resume-making tool.

466. University Crowdfunding Platform – Fundraising for student projects and research.

467. Student Debate & Public Speaking App – Virtual debate competitions and training.

468. Startup Incubation Center for Colleges – Helping student startups grow.

469. Campus Digital Notice Board – App for sharing updates, notices, and resources.

470. AI-Based Peer Learning Platform – Students helping each other through AI-driven study groups.

471. Student Hobby & Talent Platform – Showcasing student skills in music, art, and sports.

472. Gaming Video Editing Service – Editing montages and highlights for streamers.

473. Virtual Esports Host – Organize online tournaments and gaming competitions.

474. Elderly Fitness Programs – Specialized fitness classes like yoga, chair exercises, and low-impact workouts.

475. Mobile Health Check-up Services – At-home diagnostic and wellness check-ups.

476. Senior Telemedicine Platform – Virtual consultations with doctors, specialists, and mental health professionals.

477. Medication Reminder & Delivery Service – App-based reminders with automatic medicine delivery.

478. Smart Home Automation for Seniors – Installing voice-activated devices and safety sensors.

479. Elderly-Friendly Home Modification Services – Retrofitting homes with ramps, non-slip flooring, and handrails.

480. Companion Care Services – Providing trained caregivers for social interaction and emotional support.

481. 24/7 Emergency Response System – Wearable devices with SOS buttons for emergencies.

482. Short-Term Senior Care Facilities – Offering temporary care for seniors when families travel.

483. Senior-Friendly Smartphone & Tablet Training – Teaching seniors how to use technology for communication.

484. AI Voice Assistant for Seniors – Personalized AI assistants to help with reminders, entertainment, and health tracking.

485. Online Community & Social Network for Seniors – A digital platform for senior engagement and networking.

486. Cybersecurity Service for Seniors – Protecting elderly users from online scams and fraud.

487. Tech Support for Seniors – On-call or in-home tech assistance for gadgets and internet use.

488. Wheelchair & Mobility Aid Rentals – Short-term and long-term rental of wheelchairs and walkers.

489. Electric Mobility Scooters for Seniors – Developing and selling easy-to-use electric scooters.

490. Senior Travel & Vacation Planning – Assisted travel services for seniors with medical or mobility needs.

491. Memory & Cognitive Training Games – Developing brain-stimulating apps and puzzles for cognitive health.

492. Senior Hobby & Learning Classes – Art, music, gardening, and lifelong learning workshops.

493. Book Club & Audiobook Subscription for Seniors – Curated reading and audiobook services for elderly users.

494. Personalized Storytelling & Legacy Book Services – Helping seniors document their life stories for family keepsakes.

495. Elderly Event & Social Gathering Services – Organizing meetups, cultural events, and community gatherings.

496. Parenting Support Groups: Start a platform that connects parents with similar challenges, offering support groups, workshops, and resources. This community can provide a space for parents to share experiences, seek advice, and learn from one another.

497. Personalized Storybooks: Develop a service that creates customised storybooks featuring children's names and interests. These custom books can foster a love for reading while making kids feel special and engaged in the stories they read.

498. Child-Friendly Meal Prep Service: Create a meal prep service that provides healthy, kid-friendly meals that parents can easily prepare at home. This service can include recipes, pre-measured ingredients, and fun cooking activities encouraging kids to get involved in the kitchen.

499. Kids' Fitness Programs: Start a business offering fun and interactive fitness classes for kids. These programs can include dance, yoga, or sports and promote physical health while teaching children the importance of staying active.

500. Educational Subscription Boxes: Create a subscription service that delivers monthly boxes of educational toys, books, and activities tailored to different age groups. Each box can focus on a specific theme, such as science, art, or language, encouraging kids to learn while having fun.

● 60 ●

II

Special Mention: Startups of Late with Huge Success!

1. Zomato: From Food Delivery to a Tech-Driven Ecosystem

Year Founded: 2008 (but scaled significantly in the 2020s)
Founders: Deepinder Goyal and Pankaj Chaddah

Unique Story:

Zomato, originally a restaurant discovery platform, transformed into a tech-driven food delivery giant during the 2020s. The COVID-19 pandemic accelerated its growth as people relied heavily on food delivery services. Zomato expanded its offerings to include grocery delivery, subscription-based dining programs (Zomato Pro), and even drone-based delivery experiments. In 2021, Zomato went public, becoming one of India's most successful IPOs. Its ability to adapt and innovate during challenging times has made it a household name.

Key Takeaway: Diversification and adaptability are crucial for scaling a business in uncertain times.

2. BYJU'S: Revolutionizing EdTech

Year Founded: 2011 (but gained prominence in the 2020s)
Founder: Byju Raveendran

Unique Story:

BYJU capitalized on the surge in online learning during the pandemic, becoming one of the world's most valuable ed-tech companies. It offers interactive learning apps for students and has acquired several global ed-tech platforms, including WhiteHat Jr. and Aakash Educational Services. BYJU launched free live classes during the pandemic, making quality education accessible to millions. Its innovative approach to learning, combining gamification and personalized content, has redefined education in India and beyond.

Key Takeaway: Identifying a critical need (like accessible education) and scaling rapidly can lead to global success.

3. Unacademy: Democratizing Education

Year Founded: 2015 (scaled significantly in the 2020s)

Founders: Gaurav Munjal, Roman Saini, Hemesh Singh, and Sachin Gupta

Unique Story:

Unacademy started as a YouTube channel and evolved into a full-fledged online learning platform. During the pandemic, it became a lifeline for students preparing for competitive exams. The platform's live classes, interactive sessions, and affordable pricing made it a learner's favourite. It also attracted top educators, who were offered a share in the company's success. In 2020, Unacademy became a unicorn, proving that education can be accessible and profitable.

Key Takeaway: Leveraging technology to democratize access to quality education can create a massive impact.

4. Swiggy Instamart: Redefining Quick Commerce

Year Founded: 2020 (as part of Swiggy)
Parent Company: Swiggy

Unique Story:

Swiggy, known for its food delivery services, launched Swiggy Instamart in 2020 to capitalize on the growing demand for quick grocery delivery. The service promises delivery within 15-30 minutes and leverages a network of dark stores (micro-warehouses). During the pandemic, when people avoided crowded markets, Swiggy Instamart became a game-changer. Its focus on speed, convenience, and a wide product range has made it a leader in the quick commerce space.

Key Takeaway: Identifying emerging trends (like quick commerce) and executing them efficiently can lead to rapid growth.

5. Meesho: Empowering Small Businesses and Resellers

Year Founded: 2015 (gained momentum in the 2020s)
Founders: Vidit Aatrey and Sanjeev Barnwal

Unique Story:

Meesho started as a platform for small businesses and resellers to sell products on social media. It gained massive traction during the pandemic as people turned to online selling to supplement their income. Meesho's zero-commission model and focus on Tier 2 and 3 cities made it a favorite among small entrepreneurs. In 2021, Meesho became a unicorn and expanded its offerings to include grocery delivery and other categories. Its mission to democratize e-commerce for small businesses has made it a standout start-up.

Key Takeaway: Empowering underserved communities and leveraging social media can create a scalable business model.

6. PharmEasy: Revolutionizing Healthcare Access

Year Founded: 2015 (scaled significantly in the 2020s)
Founders: Dharmil Sheth, Dhaval Shah, and Dr. Harsh Parekh

Unique Story:

PharmEasy emerged as a leading online pharmacy and healthcare platform during the pandemic, addressing the critical need for accessible medicines and diagnostic services. It offers doorstep drug delivery, lab test bookings, and teleconsultations. The platform also partnered with local pharmacies to digitize their operations, creating a win-win situation for consumers and businesses. In 2021, PharmEasy became a unicorn, highlighting the growing importance of digital healthcare solutions.

Key Takeaway: Digitizing traditional industries like healthcare can create massive value for consumers and businesses.

7. CRED: Making Credit Card Payments Rewarding

Year Founded: 2018 (gained prominence in the 2020s)
Founder: Kunal Shah

Unique Story:

CRED disrupted fintech by creating a platform that rewards users for paying their credit card bills on time. It gamified the process by offering exclusive rewards, discounts, and access to premium experiences. CRED also introduced features like rent payments and credit score monitoring, making it a one-stop solution for credit card users. Its unique approach and premium branding helped it attract millions of users and achieve unicorn status in 2021.

Key Takeaway: Gamification and premium branding can turn mundane tasks (like bill payments) into engaging experiences.

8. Urban Company: Transforming Home Services

Year Founded: 2014 (scaled significantly in the 2020s)
Founders: Abhiraj Bhal, Raghav Chandra, and Varun Khaitan

Unique Story:

Urban Company (formerly UrbanClap) became a household name by offering reliable and professional home services, from cleaning and plumbing to beauty and wellness. During the pandemic, it introduced safety protocols like sanitization and contactless services, earning customer trust. The platform also empowered thousands of service professionals by providing training, tools, and a steady income. Urban Company's focus on quality and convenience has made it a leader in the home services industry.

Key Takeaway: Standardizing and professionalizing unorganized sectors can create a trusted and scalable business.

9. Razorpay: Simplifying Digital Payments for Businesses

Year Founded: 2014 (gained momentum in the 2020s)
Founders: Harshil Mathur and Shashank Kumar

Unique Story:

Razorpay began as a business payment gateway and has since expanded into a full-stack financial solutions provider. It offers services such as payroll management, lending, and neo-banking, catering to the increasing needs of Indian businesses. During the pandemic, Razorpay played a vital role in assisting small businesses with their transition to online payments. Its innovative solutions and focus on customer needs enabled it to achieve unicorn status in 2020.

Key Takeaway: Building a comprehensive ecosystem around a core product can drive long-term growth.

10. Cult.fit: Redefining Fitness and Wellness

Year Founded: 2016 (scaled significantly in the 2020s)
Founders: Mukesh Bansal and Ankit Nagori

Unique Story:

Cult.fit started as a chain of fitness centers and quickly adapted to the pandemic by pivoting to digital fitness solutions. It launched live and on-demand workout sessions, mental wellness programs, and healthy meal plans. Cult.fit's ability to combine physical and mental wellness under one platform made it a favorite among fitness enthusiasts. The company also expanded into healthcare services, offering diagnostics and teleconsultations.

Key Takeaway: Diversifying offerings and embracing digital transformation can help businesses thrive in challenging times.

III

About The Author

Dr. Dheeraj Mehrotra, is a distinguished educational leader and innovator with over three decades of experience transforming education through excellence and innovation. A recipient of the President of India's National Teacher Award (2006), he is a certified expert in Six Sigma (White and Yellow Belt), Neuro-Linguistic Programming (NLP), and Total Quality Management (TQM). His specialisation encompasses academic audits, school quality assurance and accreditation (SQAA), and implementing Kaizen and 5S in schools. As an accomplished author, Dr. Mehrotra has published over 200 books on various subjects, including computer science, artificial intelligence, digital body language, quality circles, and school management. His contributions also include the development of more than 150 free educational mobile apps for teachers, students, and parents, a feat recognised by the Limca Book of Records and the India Book of Records. Dr. Mehrotra has served as Principal at prestigious institutions such as De Indian Public School in New Delhi, NPS International School in Guwahati, and Kunwar's Global School in Lucknow. He has also held the position of Education Officer at GEMS in Gurgaon, making significant contributions to the global education community. As a premier UDEMY instructor, Dr. Mehrotra has created over 500 courses that have impacted more than 800,000 learners across 180 countries. Additionally, as the founder and president of the IoT Society of India, he advocates for technology integration in education worldwide.

www.authordheerajmehrotra.com

IV
Books By The Same Author

Scan Here
FOR QUALITY BOOKS
For Home Library for
Parents, Educators &Students